FIDE

Taylor Gaines

Published by Taylor Gaines, 2024.

FIDE

First edition. May 16, 2024.

ISBN: 979-8224160563

Written by Taylor Gaines.

The gospel is the good news of Jesus.

Two thousand years ago, a boy was born in Bethlehem, in modern day Israel. When he grew up, he said, "Repent, for the Kingdom of Heaven is at hand!". That is: turn from your life without God, and enter reality as it really is, where God is present and approachable starting today. More than that, he said he also was God, somehow, and offered the one and only path to himself.

Through his death on the cross and his resurrection three days later, he proved the trustworthiness of what he said and he accomplished the sacrifice needed to reconcile sinful man with an utterly holy and praiseworthy God, welcoming all who believe in him into adoption into his family.

Again, the Kingdom of Heaven is like treasure hidden in the field, which a man found and hid. In his joy, he goes and sells all that he has and buys that field.

Again, the Kingdom of Heaven is like a man who is a merchant seeking fine pearls, who having found one pearl of great price, he went and sold all that he had and bought it.

Matthew 13:44-46

Introduction

This book is about Jesus.

It is also about the FIRE movement, which really struck me when I first heard about it. FIRE, which stands for Financial Independence and Retire Early, is a movement based around sharing a message, evangelizing to a world which seems to value the almighty dollar above all things that there is a better way. The FIRE movement proclaims that money is just a tool, and time is the real resource you should value. And the hearers respond to that message, and either reject it and continue to live as they have, or else accept it and reorient their lives around this new understanding.

It struck me for three reasons. One, the insight that money should not be the end goal of life, but rather living, by all standards, appears very wise. And, as we shall see, the maxim "money cannot buy happiness" has been discovered and rediscovered by humanity throughout the ages. Two, I (and I do not think I am alone) am susceptible to the lure of money and the comfort it provides in the present and the security it promises for the future. I live in a wealthy country in a wealthy age where there is no reason I need to be hungry or be without shelter or be unclothed, so long as I have money. If I can find money, I can exchange it readily to meet all my basic needs. I enjoy thinking of new ways to make money, and making plans to make sure I am using my money in the best way to make even more money. And three, such pointing to the nature of reality and the radical call to change the priorities of one's life reminds me of another call I heard fairly late in my life.

This other call was the message of Jesus: that Jesus is God and died for sinners in the world like me so that we could have a relationship

4

with him. One would think that living in a wealthy nation I would have learned about one of the largest world religions and knew some of what was written in the most studied book in history, but I was mostly ignorant. I did not know who Jesus really was or what he said until I was twenty-one years old. For this reason, I began this book with a short summary of what the "good news" of Jesus is, so that if there is anyone like me who has never heard it, they will have at least heard it once, and hopefully are made curious to explore it more.

And where the FIRE movement invites its hearers to prioritize time over money, and thus change the way they live their lives, the Jesus movement says that the worship of time or money are nothing in comparison with the worship of God, and that this "life" is just the beginning of an eternal existence, and what we think we know is just a dim shadow of what truly is. The way of following Jesus is not a boring and stuffy chore necessary to eventually earn a ticket to heaven. He is not a damper on the joys of life, saying "do this, but don't do that." Rather, as he says in John 10:10, "I came that they may have life, and may have it abundantly." I figure that some people who were glad to have heard of FIRE, those who said "I wish I had known about this earlier!" and changed their lives to match their new understanding, will be similarly glad to hear the message of Jesus.

This book will reference the Bible often, which, then as an exploring non-Christian and now as a Christian, is the most helpful resource for clearing up misconceptions about what Christianity claims. These misconceptions arise from years of religious traditions and cultural norms tacked onto the name of Christianity, and basic human impulses to hurt and obtain power for oneself; these are concretions marring the clear understanding of the basics of what Jesus is saying. These disfigurements of Christianity could be, if not completely removed, made more manageable, but for a lack of reading the Bible and a lack of belief that the Bible has anything useful to say to our modern era.

When I reference the Bible, I am using the World English Bible (WEB) translation for ease of reproducibility.

In writing this, I am hoping not to write anything new. Rather, I am hoping to write something very old, but simply in a different context. J. I. Packer, a Christian, encouraged questioning the idea that, "the newer is the truer, only what is recent is decent, every shift of ground is a step forward, and every latest word must be hailed as the last word on its subject." The content of this book draws heavily upon two sources: *The Moral Vision of the New Testament* by Richard B. Hays, and *The Divine Conspiracy* by Dallas Willard. The former is an excellent resource for those interested in the greater project of how to read the words of Jesus and the writers of the New Testament and know what they are saying, and has a small section specifically on the topic of financial interdependence. The latter is an excellent resource on what it means to be a disciple of Jesus and applying what he says as if you actually believe him to be true. Both of these authors are not writing anything new, either, and are drawing upon the collected wisdom of Christians through the years, who in turn are drawing on the wisdom of Christians before them; and all are drawing upon the Bible, and so ultimately upon God.

Chapter One

The FIRE Movement

The cost of a thing is the amount of what I will call life which is required to be exchanged for it, immediately or in the long run."

— Henry David Thoreau, *Walden*

"We buy things we don't need with money we don't have to impress people we don't like."

— Chuck Palahniuk, *Fight Club*

IT WAS NOT ALWAYS TRUE that self-sufficient retirement was a concept in the mind of man. At one time, you were far more likely to die of war, famine, plague, or accident than to reach old age. When you worked, as a farmer or a sailor or a tentmaker, growing your own food or working to trade for it, you did so until your body would not allow you to do so, and then you trusted your continued care to your children and neighbors, hoping they would be able to provide for you.

Today, the respectable way to live one's life is to work for at least thirty years to forty years, or until sixty five years of age, whichever day comes first. When that day comes, which you have been dreaming about for years (and keep in mind, you have not been idle—you likely bought a house and raised a family, went on vacation, met new people and visited new places, been a productive member of society and been a reliable consumer in the economy; and, most importantly, you have been smartly saving and investing approximately 10-15% of your income every paycheck you could), your employer throws you a moderately-sized party and you do not return on the next workday. That party was your retirement party, and the day after begins your retirement. Now, you are free to pursue hobbies, sleep in, and live a life of total freedom that was denied to you while you worked to save enough money to survive independently in this freedom.

This way of living is the default. It is given to you without you even choosing. My newborn daughter was barely two weeks old, with the great adventure of life wide open before her, and she was given the gift of a check to be invested into her college fund, so that compound interest could begin its work as she was learning how to breastfeed and hold her head up with less support.

And it is a pretty funny way of living. If it was not funny, and if people did not realize it was funny, comedies such as Office Space or The Office would not exist. But why is it so funny? Is all irony funny, or is it sometimes tragic? All of our greatest inherited wisdom is univocal in saying "money cannot buy happiness". No one says having a pile of money so high you can swim in it is the ultimate goal of life, and in our stories the dragon sitting upon his treasures is never satisfied in his greed; nor is he the hero. In fact, it is often said the best things cannot be bought with money: family, friends, love, laughter, and good health can all be had for free. Obviously, to a degree, money can help you to get these things, but ask the man dying of cancer if he would not trade all he had to be cured. Many problems in life cannot be solved with money.

Time is another in this category that the FIRE movement focuses on. The movement realizes that while you can spend time for money, you cannot spend money for time. And, if people are given a choice, they would often want to spend their time doing things other than work. Time is therefore more precious, and so proponents of the movement seek to use money as a tool, going all-in with investments and frugality to retire earlier than is standard with the standard way of living.

The FIRE movement began with ideas from two popular books: *Your Money or Your Life*, a 1992 title from Vicki Robin and Joe Dominguez, and *Early Retirement Extreme*, written in 2010 by Jacob Lund Fisker. Both books describe a lifestyle of extreme savings combined with simple living so that a person can quit their job, if they desire, and money will not be a concern. These ideas were brought online and into the mainstream by bloggers, the most notable of whom is called Mr. Money Mustache.

Financial Independence

In 2012, Mr. Money Mustache published a blog titled *The Shockingly Simple Math Behind Early Retirement*. This blog describes the FIRE movement with a group of numbers that are familiar to anyone following the lifestyle. If a person saves and invests the standard 10-15% of their income as they work to create a nest egg for retirement, they will have to work for 43-51 years to continue living with their same spending habits into retirement. That sounds like a lot, but that is what many people do. If someone retires at 65, these numbers describe a career that starts at age 22, which is reasonable for someone who went to college.

But these numbers are not interesting, or else somewhat depressing, for someone interested in the FIRE lifestyle. Some surprising and exciting numbers emerge when the percent income saved and invested increases. If 50% of someone's income is saved, a person can instead retire after only 17 years of working. This 22 year old would instead be 39 when he retires, and with the same ability as the 65 year old to pay for his living expenses in retirement. If someone can save 75% of their income, they can instead retire in only 7 years! These numbers hold true regardless of if a person is earning $1 million, $100,00, or $10,000 per year. The difference comes in that those earning more (and saving more) can have a higher standard of living, while those saving less will live with a lower standard. But there is a bit of a floor among low earners, where most low earners cannot save 75% of their take home income while also paying for food and housing. Following the FIRE movement is an easier task for higher earners able to live modestly.

Another number familiar in the FIRE community is 4%. This number is the "safe" withdrawal rate per year from a retirement nest egg with the goal of not running out of money within your lifetime. The number 4%, as opposed to 3% or 5% or 9%, is based on historic data in the United States. With 4%, a person must save 25 times their expected yearly expenses in retirement before they can stop working. The length of "lifetime" does not matter too much in this calculation. Theoretically, the nest egg might never run out. This is because in the FIRE movement you have this money invested in some vehicle (for example, the stock market or real estate) that hopefully grows yearly at some rate above that of inflation. If that rate of growth is high enough, it should never run out. If this is difficult to comprehend, it may be helpful to think of this not as an investment you want to grow, but as a debt you wish would shrink: if you have a student loan or mortgage with a very high interest rate, it is possible to never be able to pay off that loan. All of your payments might be going to the interest, and the principal is not decreasing, and so the principal generates the same amount of interest or more again.

And these numbers are interesting because they truly exemplify financial independence. These numbers assume there is no other source of income following the retirement date. There is no salary, even from part-time work. There is no social security. There are no inheritances, and not even birthday presents. Looking at this, it is a great wonder that anyone can manage to need 50 years of paychecks to retire!

Two factors stand out as immediate culprits for this difference between the apparent mathematical ease of an early and comfortable retirement and the reality of many people's financial situation: a person's income and a person's ability to save. FIRE proponents point to this second reason as the most important thing. Most people, they say, spend money on things that are not important. And this is not necessarily one person judging what is important for another, but rather one person helping another person evaluate what is important through a new lens. For example, does a person need to pay the premium expense for a brand new car? Or, could they get by with an old car, or else a bike, if it meant they could retire a few years earlier? Or would they go on that weeklong vacation, or pay for a year of cable television, or buy a daily coffee, if they could instead trade it for time? By all means, perhaps there is some person that would not trade that daily coffee for anything, even if the only sacrifice they would experience is instead making coffee more frugally at home. Most people would assume there might be something more valuable within an extra and earlier year of retirement than in made-to-order coffees which are consumed and pass into the sewer, but perhaps that is not always true.

Retire Early

FIRE lifestyle proponents would say most critiques about this movement are not about "financial independence", which is mathematical and concrete, but are instead related to the concept of "retire early". So, we will first look at this concept from the perspective of the critics, and examine why FIRE proponents say these are not valid but are rather misconceptions.

One such critique is based on the idea that people who retire have worked hard and earned it, and so, if someone has only worked for 10 or 15 years, they clearly have not earned it yet. They are accused of being lazy.

Or, they are accused of being stupid. Or if not stupid, then of taking on a stupid amount of risk. How can someone stop working with half of their life remaining and expect to have enough money to survive? The calculation for how much money needed to retire is based on needing a moderate return on one's investments. But, what if the stock market crashes and takes years to recover, or else never recovers, or inflation rockets to the moon? What if there is civil war? What if we move away from money as we know it and move to some kind of digital currency, or else return to a system of bartering goods and services? The future is unknown, and so having a longer retirement, where one unexpected event can wipe out your savings, is more risky than having a shorter one.

But if they are not stupid, they are greedy and have a cold, shriveled, and laughless heart like Ebeneezer Scrooge. Critics see those who follow the FIRE movement as people only invested in themselves. The stereotype is of someone who you invite out to a restaurant for dinner or drinks, but they decline in order to save money; or, if you can convince or trick them to go, they order a water and eat chips and bread. At Christmas, they give you some unwanted hand-made item or something obviously regifted in order to save themselves money, but at the expense of not giving you what you would actually want. They are eager to share car rides with you as a cost savings measure, but unfortunately don't own a car and so can't return the favor. And then, once enough money is saved to enter an early retirement, they must become even more tight-fisted because they have no reliable income to buffer.

Another critique, unrelated to the possibility of the plan working, is the fairness of it. The critics say only relatively wealthy people can afford to save such a large percentage of their income, while those who live paycheck to paycheck have no chance to participate. Therefore, to follow the FIRE lifestyle, instead of, I suppose, donating one's would-be savings to charities attempting to alleviate poverty, is unethical and unjust.

And, due to all of this, the person following the FIRE movement lives an unhappy life devoid of meaning.

But are these critiques valid? Perhaps someone who held a job for a long time did it because it was especially easy and they liked the guaranteed paycheck, while the person working and saving in the FIRE lifestyle was working objectively harder. In terms of taking on risk, no one—literally, no one—knows the future, but who is more prepared for the possibilities: the average person, or someone who has researched and dedicated their life to the FIRE lifestyle? In terms of being greedy, isn't everyone capable of being greedy? The default position is to care more about oneself than about others, and it is not abnormal or unexpected to do so. Why is someone who invests a larger portion of their income for the future greedier than someone who uses that same money to buy things for themselves in the present? Why are FIRE proponents, attempting to create wealth for themselves, uniquely blamed for not being also able to create wealth for others?

But perhaps the biggest rebuttal to the critique of the FIRE movement is related to the claim that followers of FIRE are not happy or can't lead meaningful lives. They would say those who make these claims misunderstand FIRE, or are distracted by the phrase 'retire early'. FIRE is centered around achieving financial independence so that there is time to seek happiness, self-fulfillment, and meaning (and these words all mean something slightly different, though of course there may be overlap: for example, if someone finds the most meaning in optimizing happiness) in the life they live. Happiness or meaning is the end goal. Therefore, if the choices you are making and the anxieties you are fretting over are causing you to be less happy, you are doing FIRE wrong. If you see frugality as the end goal rather than a tool to reach the end goal, you will suffer from resentment towards your self-imposed deprivation. Many people, first excited by the prospects of FIRE, fall away for this reason. But other FIRE proponents would say these people never really understood what FIRE is all about.

So after looking at what the critics say, what would someone who actually knows what FIRE is say about retiring early? There are many choices on what retirement will look like because it is supposed to be optimized for the individual. "Retirement" is spending your time as you would want to spend it. Perhaps some people would choose to spend their Monday through Friday in an office setting for eight hours per day, and FIRE would allow you to continue doing that, but it does not require you to. Maybe retirement looks like having a house paid off so that you can live simply and enjoy hobbies like art, music, or sports. Perhaps it allows you to start a second career, possibly one that is lower paying, or gives you time to learn something you never had time to before. Perhaps you can travel and see the world while your body is still young and you can enjoy it more. Maybe you would rather spend your time volunteering with an organization that cannot afford to pay you, but now you are financially independent so you do not require payment to survive. People in the FIRE movement can obviously still find meaning in their daily lives. Rather than being given the purpose of waking up in order to work five days per week for forty years, they instead can make their own.

And the money needed for retirement doesn't look the same for all followers of FIRE. There is not one choice but rather a spectrum of lifestyle choices, so obviously recognized within the FIRE community there are names for them. There is Lean FIRE, which requires a smaller amount of savings and therefore a much more frugal lifestyle in retirement. There is Fat FIRE, where someone seeks to retire with a fat stack of cash and live a life of relative luxury and comfort and they have the time to enjoy the money they have earned. In the middle of these is something called barista FIRE, where the retiree intends to work a part time job like a coffee maker in order to have some income, enjoy the camaraderie of working, and to have a routine, while also being able to have plenty of time to do other activities.

Looking at this description of what "retire early" means in FIRE, here is a bold thought: did Mother Theresa embrace the FIRE lifestyle? She arranged her life in a way that money was not a hindrance to her doing what she really wanted to do: living with and caring for the dying poor in

Calcutta, India and other locations in service to Jesus Christ. This might be considered a "lean FIRE", to understate it. And she was certainly subject to plenty of criticism, just like other proponents of the FIRE movement. Besides pushback to her stances on abortion and divorce, she was criticized for giving poor care to the poor, perhaps caring for peoples' spiritual needs (or what she believed to be their spiritual needs) without really alleviating their physical lack. But what can you do with such people? Surely, those critics live lives above reproach and with far more meaning, and do far more for the poor? Perhaps Mother Theresa should have held an office job and regularly contributed part of her income to care for the poor? Someone still might critique her for that.

The "retire early" part of the FIRE movement is deeply controversial, but most proponents have learned to tune out the critics. Criticisms against the movement appear to be endless. Depending on who is speaking, those who choose to follow FIRE are either foolish, or else too smart and are taking advantage of "the system". Everyday, people are taking advantage of and being taken advantage of by the system. In light of that, the FIRE movement seems to be a reasonable and well-thought out choice.

The Bible on FIRE

But this book is based on the premise that the Bible shows a better vision for what to do with your money and what to do with your time. That itself is premised, somewhat presumptuously, on the idea that most people have a distorted understanding of reality, and therefore have a distorted sense of priorities and values, and so they need to be awoken to how things really are and have their heart transformed to be oriented to love the right things. C.S. Lewis, the author of the Chronicles of Narnia and much more, said in discussing inculcating these proper loves,

> "It would seem that Our Lord finds our desires not too strong, but too weak. We are half-hearted creatures, fooling about with drink and sex and

ambition when infinite joy is offered us, like an ignorant child who wants to go on making mud pies in a slum because he cannot imagine what is meant by the offer of a holiday at the sea. We are far too easily pleased."

— C.S. Lewis, *The Weight of Glory, and Other Addresses*

But before allowing the Bible to speak about these infinite joys on its own terms, it is fair for it to first respond to the claims of the FIRE movement. Where does it agree, and where does it disagree?

Obviously, a book whose parts were written multiple thousands of years ago does not speak to something called the "FIRE movement", a term coined only recently in history. But we share the questions at the heart of the FIRE movement with ancient civilizations; despite our technological advances, humans ourselves really have not changed that much. Money existed then, as it exists today; what should we do with it? What does "the good life" look like, or what does it mean to be a good person? The book of Proverbs is a good place to start to look for wisdom, full of pithy statements which seem to be true across the generations. These verses and the messages contained within them might look familiar to FIRE proponents.

He becomes poor who works with a lazy hand,

but the hand of the diligent brings wealth.

He who gathers in summer is a wise son,

but he who sleeps during the harvest is a son who

causes shame.

— Proverbs 10:4-5

He who tills his land shall have plenty of bread,

but he who chases fantasies is void of understanding.

— Proverbs 12:11

A good man leaves an inheritance to his children's children,

but the wealth of the sinner is stored for the righteous.

— Proverbs 13:22

The plans of the diligent surely lead to profit;

and everyone who is hasty surely rushes to poverty.

— Proverbs 21:5

He who loves pleasure will be a poor man.

He who loves wine and oil won't be rich.

— Proverbs 21:17

The message is obvious: those who work hard and diligently (that is, sharply and with a plan) will be prosperous and able to care for themselves and others, while those who are lazy or squander their wealth on short-lived or frivolous things will be poor. Similar morals can be found in the fables of Aesop or other less well-known tales in culture and time (notable exceptions are the Grimm fairy tales, in which it seems the only choices in life are to be maimed or eaten, or to avoid being maimed or eaten, and the Disney remakes, in which the moral is be one's "true self" and all your desires will come true [unless you are the villain, then it is bad to be true to oneself]).

Those who are not Christians (and think them foolish) may smile at the irony of Proverbs 12:11 ("chasing fantasies is void of understanding"), and some may also appreciate the irony that they think the statement is wise.

Ecclesiastes is another book of the Bible read for wisdom, and it has similar pro-FIRE verses (though we will also spend time with Ecclesiates in other sections).

Give a portion to seven, yes, even to eight;

for you don't know what evil will be on the earth.

— Ecclesiastes 11:2

The idea here is similar to the aphorism "don't place all of your eggs in one basket", and is one familiar to the FIRE community. In seeking financial independence, don't rely only on your job, which may be terminated, or your pension, which may run out, or Social Security, which will run out or be modified from what it currently offers, but also support yourself with passive income sources, manage real estate, or work a side hustle. Or perhaps it is saying that the Bible supports the idea of investing in mutual funds rather than individual equities to diversify risk.

In the world in which the Bible was written, as stated earlier, the idea of retirement was an oddity. However, there are some verses which suggest the beginning of the FIRE movement, pointing specifically towards the RE portion of the acronym. For example, in Hebrews:

> There remains therefore a Sabbath rest for the people of God. For he who has entered into his rest has himself also rested from his works, as God did from his. Let's therefore give diligence to enter into that rest...

— Hebrews 4:9-11a

If the selective editing of the last passage did not clue you in, some of these verses I chose to advocate for FIRE are more tongue in cheek than others and stretched beyond their intended purpose, and the meaning of some passages are outright being tortured for my stated purpose and for the sake of a point.

Like all written words, to best understand them you should try to understand the context of the world in which they were written, the context of the words around them, and the intent of the author and how they wanted their audience to understand them. Obviously, this small booklet cannot provide all the understanding necessary to think about this topic, but I hope it begins to point in the right direction.

How are we to judge what the best interpretation of a passage is, or if there is such a thing as a bad interpretation? As we said, the Bible is the most studied book in the world. The book mentioned in the introduction, *The Moral Vision of the New Testament*, provides a helpful roadmap for beginners in the task of reading, interpreting, and acting on the commands and concepts in the writings of the New Testament. Well-informed and well-meaning Christians still disagree about various issues pertaining to Christianity and how to interpret different passages, in the same way that well-informed and well-meaning scientists disagree about the interpretation of different scientific findings. And yet, in spite of this, chemistry has overtaken alchemy as a valuable tool for understanding the nature of reality. It has done this by sticking to a method which can test certain truth claims and decide if they are true or false; when scientists disagree, they can often settle these disagreements by performing tests, and are able to change their minds based on the results of these tests. Sometimes, scientists must exercise humility when there is some truth claim we cannot yet cannot ever evaluate via the scientific method; how much more so for Christians in evaluating the Bible or critiquing their Christian brothers and sisters.

But what are some of the more alchemical ways of using the Bible, ways we know are foolish to pursue? We should not treat the Bible like fodder for a ransom letter, cutting and pasting parts as we choose to make it say what we wish it said. Nor like a Magic 8-Ball, where we ask a question and are satisfied with the first answer we receive, not wanting to shake it again just in case the answer changes. Nor like a game of darts, opening to a random page and slamming our fingers down to find out what the Bible is trying to teach us this day. Bible scholars even have names for the right and wrong ways of interpretation. Exegesis is the interpretation of the Bible in its correct context, trying to allow it to speak for itself. This is what we should try to do. Eisegesis is the word for illegitimately reading your own ideas into the Bible, and we should try to avoid this misuse.

The most harrowing example of the danger of misusing the Bible comes from the Bible itself. Matthew 4 and Luke 4 both tell a story early in Jesus' work where he is tempted by "the tempter" (Satan, the devil) to disobey commands that God had laid down millennia before, and he uses the Bible to do it! The book of James shows a similar situation where having knowledge of what the Bible says does not necessarily mean having wisdom about what the Bible means ("You believe that God is one. You do well. The demons also believe, and shudder." — James 2:19). But in the temptation of Jesus, his tool in resisting the devil is knowing the Bible also, and he uses words from the same scriptures that he is being attacked with to defend himself.

But since we are not Jesus, how are we supposed to know which interpretation is correct? Today, in which we are all a product of the common philosophies of the previous generation, whether we want to admit it or not, a common idea is that someone's interpretation is that which is most beneficial to them. For example, in the past slave owners in the United States used the Bible as justification for why they should be allowed to own slaves, why they cannot run away, and why it is right for a Christian to beat them. It certainly seems in this case like the Bible justified that which they already believed. And yet, other Christians interpreted the Bible as saying it is unjust to kidnap or buy and enslave another human being. It could be said there was some benefit to these people for holding this interpretation; perhaps they earned high social status for holding such an elite opinion? I don't think this was the case, looking at history. I think these people were ostracized, beaten, and killed for threatening another person's means of money and power. So the only benefit to them was holding to the truth of what the Bible says, which is, admittedly, complex. Examine the short letter Philemon, which is less than one page in the Bible, for an example of what I mean by this. Then, consider what else the rest of the Bible says, as well.

Today, people discuss "my truth" and "your truth". The authors of the Bible did not intend this. While a predecessor to this ideology may have existed in other cultures in the times when the Bible was written, the authors of the Bible believed in "the truth".

Test all things, and hold firmly that which is good.

— 1 Thessalonians 5:21

Of course, my claim that they believe in "the truth" may simply be "my truth", as the slave owners believed Christians can own slaves, and so you need not read the Bible as if such a thing as "the truth" really exists. Such thinking is poison to all it touches, termites to a foundation of knowledge, and ironically has the exact same effect of self-justifying someone's ideas as the thinking claims to critique. Sometimes, people do justify themselves for their own benefit. We must allow that sometimes, though, someone holds an interpretation because they actually believe it is true, even if it does not benefit them. Holding the cynical view that all claims to truth are actually veiled bids for power will wreak havoc on your ability to think logically, build friendships, or assign objective value or beauty to anything.

Briefly, the defenses against both blatantly wrong interpretations or the idea that interpretations are essentially meaningless and unknowably true are the same: read the Bible to survey what it actually says; read books such as the one recommended above to help think through how to synthesize what the Bible says; be part of a church community (a group of Christians) who welcomes your questions and can help provide answers for them, displaying the diligence and humility of scientists who have some tools to uncover truth but not all of them. There are people seeking the truth who work with others to find that truth, and there are people who want to beguile you into parting with your money to finance their newest private jet, or rile you into a frenzy of fear or outrage to advocate for their pet political project. Both groups of people exist among those calling themselves Christians. I recommend finding those in the first group (and it is possible to find them).

That was quite a detour in examining what the Bible says positively about FIRE. But it was necessary to arrive at this conclusion: many of the principles of FIRE are good (hard work, as opposed to thievery or fraud, is good), but it does not specifically advocate for the totalizing lifestyle changes asked for by the FIRE lifestyle (working to save a large amount of your money in order to retire from working).

We will now begin a brief survey of any Biblical passages that seem to specifically discourage following the FIRE lifestyle, but it will be brief. If we have gained anything from the detour, one thing to consider is that it is inappropriate (or at least, truncated) to ask of the Bible (like a Magic 8-Ball), "So what should I think about the FIRE lifestyle?" Rather, a more complete answer can be gained from reading the Bible for its intended purpose, and surely it will answer one of the biggest questions everyone has, which is, "How should I live my life?"

Starting again in Proverbs,

> The rich man's wealth is his strong city...
>
> — Proverbs 18:11a

Well that doesn't sound so opposed to FIRE...

> ...like an unscalable wall in his own imagination.
>
> — Proverbs 18:11b

Oh. And similarly,

> Don't weary yourself to be rich.

In your wisdom, show restraint.

Why do you set your eyes on that which is not?

For it certainly sprouts wings like an eagle and flies in

the sky.

— Proverbs 23:4-5

And in Ecclesiastes,

Then I returned and saw vanity under the sun. There is one who is alone, and he has neither son nor brother. There is no end to all of his labor, neither are his eyes satisfied with wealth. "For whom then, do I labor and deprive my soul of enjoyment?" This also is vanity. Yes, it is a miserable business.

— Ecclesiastes 4:7-8

He who loves silver shall not be satisfied with silver; nor he who loves abundance, with increase: this also is vanity. When goods increase, those who eat them are increased; and what advantage is there to its owner, except to feast on them with his eyes?

The sleep of a laboring man is sweet, whether he eats little or much; but the abundance of the rich will not allow him to sleep.

— Ecclesiastes 5:10-12

But the most direct counter to the FIRE movement comes from a story that Jesus spoke, in which the character in the story is shown to be foolish for dedicating his life trying to store up wealth in order to retire and planning for a future which is not guaranteed.

He spoke a parable to them, saying, "The ground of a certain rich man produced abundantly. He reasoned within himself, saying, 'What will I do, because I don't have room to store my crops?' He said, 'This is what I will do. I will pull down my barns, build bigger ones, and there I will store all my grain and my goods. I will tell my soul, "Soul, you have many goods laid up for many years. Take your ease, eat, drink, and be merry."'

"But God said to him, 'You foolish one, tonight your soul is required of you. The things which you have prepared—whose will they be?' So is he who lays up treasure for himself, and is not rich toward God."

— Luke 12:16-21

FIDE: An Alternative to FIRE

The previous parable from the book of Luke ends with a moral; the story about the failure of the man following what looks to be the FIRE lifestyle was not the end goal, but rather an analogy to prove another point. We will discuss what this point is in more depth in the third chapter. Briefly, the point is this: whether you follow FIRE or not does not matter. Having wealth or being poor does not make you more or less "righteous" or "good". Rather, the disposition of your heart does. In *A Christmas Carol*, the heart of Ebeneezer Scrooge seems transformed from the beginning of the story to the end, and yet at the end he is still very wealthy.

And so, I will again claim that the Bible does not speak directly to FIRE. I will claim that it offers an alternative, not constrained by the language or ideas of the FIRE movement but crashing through it with its own vision of the world. Where the FIRE movement seeks to peel back the scales and lift the fog of its followers, showing that they do not have to live a life defined by the norms of a lifestyle defined by work, the Bible blasts a trumpet and crashes with thunder, proclaiming an even more earth-shattering message.

Controversially, I will say that the message of the FIRE movement is more like blowing into a kazoo at a crowded and noisy party. I do not think it is drastically different from the "normal" message of how to live one's life. Its claim is only a difference in degree, not of kind. While normal, reasonable, and unconverted people are supposed to save 10-15% of their income for retirement, FIRE proponents are supposed to save 50-75%, but both groups exist on the same scale. People look to others far below them on the scale, saying, "don't you see that if you just save more, you can retire earlier and live a life less concerned with money?", while people look to those far above them on the scale, saying, "don't you see that if you just saved a little less, you could enjoy more and live a life less concerned with money?" The message of the Bible is totally different, and concern with money is not its main concern.

I chose FIDE as a name to summarize this message, playfully competing for space with the marketing power and lifestyle demands of FIRE. FIDE stands for Financial Interdependence and Discipleship Everyday, the first half answering the question, "What does the Bible say I should do with my money?", and the second half answering the question, "How do I do it?" This is all premised on the idea that the Bible is a trustworthy source and has something intelligent to say on these topics. *Fide* is also Latin for faith, as in the Reformation-era doctrine *justificatio sola fide* (meaning the belief that Christians are justified by faith in Jesus alone, apart from needing to "be good" or "do good works"), or in the more common or legal phrase *bonafide*, meaning "in good faith" or "genuine". Like all good Latin, no one knows how to pronounce it, whether it rhymes with D-Day or with an ocean tide.

Faith is described in the Bible as the "assurance of things hoped for, proof of things not seen." (Hebrews 11:1) The rest of the chapter Hebrews 11 goes on to describe various people whose stories are told in the Old Testament who showed faith by trusting that a promise would be fulfilled, even if they themselves have not yet seen its fulfillment. And yet they still had reason to believe based on what had happened previously.

Faith to non-believers is a bit of a mystical and abstract concept, but those who follow FIRE also have faith. They have faith that their investments in the stock market will continue to grow at approximately a 10% annual rate of return based on historical rates. This is a strong anchor when economic recessions or depressions occur. Without faith in this growth, their entire plan to retire early and live off of the growth of a nest egg would be foolish. Their plan would never work, and they would be missing out on other ways of living their life to chase a fantasy. All people have faith that the sun will rise tomorrow, and that gravity will continue to work as it always has, and that the earth's magnetic field will exist and allow our planet to hold an atmosphere and protect us from solar radiation. People make plans as if this is true, planting gardens and getting married and having children, though no one can guarantee the earth will always be hospitable, and humanity's best estimates say that one day it will not be. Most FIRE proponents specifically do not have faith in Social Security to provide for them in their retirement based on looking at the evidence, and so change their lifestyle to create something they think they can rely on more. But everyone knows no one can really see the future. We can only make good guesses based on what we know and what we have seen in the past.

The next two chapters are my good guesses about what to do with each of the two parts of FIDE.

Summary

- The FIRE movement is about spreading the news of saving more money and making lifestyle changes in order to allow for a meaningful life of your choosing

- The FIRE movement is misunderstood by its critics and has been successfully undertaken by many

- The Bible has both good and bad things to say about the FIRE movement, but ultimately shares a different message

Questions for thinking

1. Do the critics of the FIRE movement make any good points? Which is the strongest critique?
2. Is the FIRE movement evangelistic in the same way Christianity is (i.e., are believers encouraged to share the good news with others who do not yet know it)?
3. Is the FIRE movement immoral? Does the Bible say the FIRE movement is off-limits to Christians?

Chapter Two

Financial Interdependence

The multitude of those who believed were of one heart and soul. Not one of them claimed that anything of the things which he possessed was his own, but they had all things in common. With great power, the apostles gave their testimony of the resurrection of the Lord Jesus. Great grace was on them all. For neither was there among them any who lacked, for as many as were owners of lands or houses sold them, and brought the proceeds of the things that were sold, and laid them at the apostles' feet, and distribution was made to each, according as anyone had need.

— Acts 4:32-35

HOW TO HANDLE MONEY is not the main message of the Bible, but it does show up frequently. Issues surrounding money are discussed from Genesis to Revelation. Money is the most frequent topic or tool for analogy in the parables of Jesus. And money is undoubtedly one of the most important topics for many people today, though I am guessing that it is not because of how frequently it is mentioned in the Bible.

The Spirit of the Times

Many, willingly or unwillingly, organize their lives around money. But it makes sense. Even if you do not value money itself, many valuable things can be bought with money. The American Dream is based on using money to own a house, provide for a family, and retire comfortably. FIRE proponents leverage this to the extreme, hoping to use money so efficiently that retirement and life goals can be achieved even earlier than normal.

People would say they are not organizing their lives around money, but do their actions or thoughts betray them? How many of their waking hours are spent making money, or traveling to a place where they can make money? How often do they devote time to learning a new skill or field of knowledge for the love of it or the love of knowledge, rather than as a resume builder to advance their career? When they lay awake at night unable to sleep, how often is it due to worrying over money problems, versus something else? Do they spend time investing in their relationships more than they spend time investing for their retirement?

But is this fair? Can someone only claim to not be concerned primarily with money if they live as a homeless nomad, eschewing money and trading for all they need through bartering goods and services? I am not claiming this. I am rather asking people to try to examine their own hearts more stringently than they might otherwise. What are you really placing your faith in? To put it another way, if tomorrow all of your money and wealth were to disappear, how would you react? Would your life be drastically changed? Would you lose sleep? Would you consider suicide? Would you be even mildly discomfited? The degree to which you are worried may show something about how much you really trust in money, as opposed to trusting in other things. I tell you I know people who would be totally unphased because I have seen them in this exact situation. But we are not all perfected yet in this. Is it worth pursuing this perfection, where we do not trust in money one bit? Let us survey what the Bible has to say.

A Brief Review of the Bible on Money

Listed below are a few ways of thinking about and using money which seem to show up repeatedly in the Bible, in both commandments and as narratives. Ideally, some familiarity on the readers' part with the texts exists or is sought out to verify I am fairly and reasonably exegeting these thematic principles.

The Bible tells us where money and wealth come from:

> ...and lest you say in your heart, "My power and the might of my hand has gotten me this wealth." But you shall remember Yahweh your God, for it is he who gives you power to get wealth, that he may establish his covenant which he swore to your fathers, as it is today.

> — Deuteronomy 8:17-18

> Every man also to whom God has given riches and wealth, and has given him power to eat of it, and to take his portion, and to rejoice in his labor—this is the gift of God. For he shall not often reflect on the days of his life; because God occupies him with the joy of his heart.

> — Ecclesiastes 5:19-20

> In the day of prosperity be joyful, and in the day of adversity consider; yes, God has made the one side by side with the other, to the end that man should not find out anything after him.

> — Ecclesiastes 7:14

And so it makes sense that if money comes from God, it is not inherently wrong to have it. Genesis 47 tells the story of Joseph who used his position of great power and wealth (and it is interesting to see how he gained it) to provide for Egypt and surrounding nations (including Israel) in a time of great famine. Job is the story of the richest man of his time, who is deemed righteous and unrighteous for reasons unrelated to how much money he held.

> His possessions also were seven thousand sheep, three thousand camels, five hundred yoke of oxen, five hundred female donkeys, and a very great household; so that this man was the greatest of all the children of the east.

> — Job 1:3

But there are also warnings that money gained is certain ways is not the same as money earned honestly:

You shall not steal.

— Exodus 20:15

You shall not covet your neighbor's house. You shall not covet your neighbor's wife, nor his male servant, nor his female servant, nor his ox, nor his donkey, nor anything that is your neighbor's.

— Exodus 20:17

Wealth gained dishonestly dwindles away,

but he who gathers by hand makes it grow.

— Proverbs 13:11

He who increases his wealth by excessive interest

gathers it for one who has pity on the poor.

— Proverbs 28:8

Let him who stole steal no more; but rather let him labor, producing with his hands something that is good, that he may have something to give to him who has need.

— Ephesians 4:28

The Bible tells us how much we should trust in money:

Then I saw all the labor and achievement that is the envy of a man's neighbor. This also is vanity and a striving after wind.

— Ecclesiastes 4:4

For man also doesn't know his time. As the fish that are taken in an evil net, and as the birds that are caught in the snare, even so are the sons of men snared in an evil time, when it falls suddenly on them.

— Ecclesiastes 9:12

Don't lay up treasures for yourselves on the earth, where moth and rust consume, and where thieves break through and steal; but lay up for yourselves treasures in heaven, where neither moth nor rust consume, and where thieves don't break through and steal; for where your treasure is, there your heart will be also.

— Matthew 6:19-21

If I have made gold my hope, and have said to the fine gold, 'You are my confidence;'

If I have rejoiced because my wealth was great, and because my hand had gotten much;

if I have seen the sun when it shined, or the moon moving in splendor,

and my heart has been secretly enticed, and my hand threw a kiss from my mouth,

this also would be an iniquity to be punished by the judges; for I should have denied the God who is above.

— Job 13:24-28

But let the brother in humble circumstances glory in his high position; and the rich, in that he is made humble, because like the flower in the grass, he will pass away. For the sun arises with the scorching wind and withers the grass, and the flower in it falls, and the beauty of its appearance perishes. So the rich man will also fade away in his pursuits.

— James 1:9-11

The merchants of the earth weep and mourn over her, for no one buys their merchandise any more: merchandise of gold, silver, precious stones, pearls, fine linen, purple, silk, scarlet, all expensive wood, every vessel of ivory, every vessel made of most precious wood, and of brass, and iron, and marble; and cinnamon, incense, perfume, frankincense, wine, olive oil, fine flour, wheat, sheep, horses, chariots, and people's bodies and souls. The fruits which your soul lusted after have been lost to you. All things that were dainty and sumptuous have perished from you, and you will find them no more at all. The merchants of these things, who were made rich by her, will stand far away for the fear of her torment, weeping and mourning, saying, 'Woe, woe, the great city, she who was dressed in fine linen, purple, and scarlet, and decked with gold and precious stones and pearls! For in an hour such great riches are made desolate.' Every ship master, and everyone who sails anywhere, and mariners, and as many as gain their living by sea, stood far away, and cried out as they looked at the smoke of her burning, saying, 'What is like the great city?' They cast dust on their heads, and cried, weeping and mourning, saying, 'Woe, woe, the great city, in which all who had their ships in the sea were made rich by reason of her great wealth!' For she is made desolate in one hour.

— Revelation 18:11-17

The Bible tells us what dangers lie in misunderstanding the above passages describing where money comes from and how much to trust in it:

Remove far from me falsehood and lies.

Give me neither poverty nor riches.

Feed me with the food that is needful for me,

lest I be full, deny you, and say, 'Who is Yahweh?'

or lest I be poor, and steal,

and so dishonor the name of my God.

— Proverbs 30:8-9

Others are those who are sown among the thorns. These are those who have heard the word, and the cares of this age, and the deceitfulness of riches, and the lusts of other things entering in choke the word, and it becomes unfruitful.

— Mark 4:18-19

Jesus looked around, and said to his disciples, "How difficult it is for those who have riches to enter into God's Kingdom!"

The disciples were amazed at his words. But Jesus answered again, "Children, how hard it is for those who trust in riches to enter into God's Kingdom! It is easier for a camel to go through a needle's eye than for a rich man to enter into God's Kingdom."

They were exceedingly astonished, saying to him, "Then who can be saved?"

Jesus, looking at them, said, "With men it is impossible, but not with God, for all things are possible with God."

— Mark 10:23-27

No servant can serve two masters, for either he will hate the one, and love the other; or else he will hold to one, and despise the other. You aren't able to serve God and Mammon.

— Luke 16:13

For the love of money is a root of all kinds of evil. Some have been led astray from the faith in their greed, and have pierced themselves through with many sorrows.

— 1 Timothy 6:10

And not just offering warnings about the dangers of trusting in money, the Bible casts a positive vision for how to think about work:

Therefore I saw that there is nothing better than that a man should rejoice in his works; for that is his portion: for who can bring him to see what will be after him?

— Ecclesiastes 7:14

Whatever your hand finds to do, do it with your might; for there is no work, nor plan, nor knowledge, nor wisdom, in Sheol, where you are going.

— Ecclesiastes 9:10

And whatever you do, work heartily, as for the Lord, and not for men, knowing that from the Lord you will receive the reward of the inheritance; for you serve the Lord Christ.

— Colossians 3:23-24

There seems to be a major theme encouraging believers not to be bothered or made anxious by money matters:

When the dew that lay had gone, behold, on the surface of the wilderness was a small round thing, small as the frost on the ground. When the children of Israel saw it, they said to one another, "What is it?" For they didn't know what it was. Moses said to them, "It is the bread which Yahweh has given you to eat. This is the thing which Yahweh has commanded: 'Gather of it everyone according to his eating; an omer a head, according to the number of your persons, you shall take it, every man for those who are in his tent.'" The children of Israel did so, and some gathered more, some less. When they measured it with an omer, he who gathered much had nothing over, and he who gathered little had no lack. They each gathered according to his eating.

— Exodus 16:14-18

It is vain for you to rise up early,

to stay up late,

eating the bread of toil,

for he gives sleep to his loved ones.

— Psalm 127:2

For though the fig tree doesn't flourish,

nor fruit be in the vines;

the labor of the olive fails,

the fields yield no food;

the flocks are cut off from the fold,

and there is no herd in the stalls:

yet I will rejoice in Yahweh.

I will be joyful in the God of my salvation!

— Habakkuk 3:17-18

Give us today our daily bread.

Forgive us our debts,

as we also forgive our debtors.

— Matthew 6:11-12, and follow with Matthew 6:24-34

Heal the sick, cleanse the lepers, and cast out demons. Freely you received, so freely give. Don't take any gold, silver, or brass in your money belts.

— Matthew 10:8-9

Don't be afraid, little flock, for it is your Father's good pleasure to give you the Kingdom. Sell that which you have, and give gifts to the needy. Make for yourselves purses which don't grow old, a treasure in the heavens that doesn't fail, where no thief approaches, neither moth destroys. For where your treasure is, there will your heart be also.

— Luke 12:32-34

My God will supply every need of yours according to his riches in glory in Christ Jesus.

— Philippians 4:19

But having food and clothing, we will be content with that.

— 1 Timothy 6:8

Charge those who are rich in this present world that they not be arrogant, nor have their hope set on the uncertainty of riches, but on the living God, who richly provides us with everything to enjoy; that they do good, that they be rich in good works, that they be ready to distribute, willing to share; laying up in store for themselves a good foundation against the time to come, that they may lay hold of eternal life.

— 1 Timothy 6:17-19

Be free from the love of money, content with such things as you have, for he has said, "I will in no way leave you, neither will I in any way forsake you." So that with good courage we say,

"The Lord is my helper. I will not fear.

What can man do to me?"

— Hebrews 13:5-6

There also seems to be a major theme to give special care to the poor, especially those oppressed by the wicked:

When you reap the harvest of your land, you shall not wholly reap the corners of your field, neither shall you gather the gleanings of your harvest. You shall not glean your vineyard, neither shall you gather the fallen grapes of your vineyard. You shall leave them for the poor and for the foreigner. I am Yahweh your God.

— Leviticus 19:9-10

If your brother has become poor, and his hand can't support himself among you, then you shall uphold him. He shall live with you like an alien and a temporary resident. Take no interest from him or profit; but fear your God, that your brother may live among you. You shall not lend him your money at interest, nor give him your food for profit.

— Leviticus 25:35-37

Better is a little that the righteous has, than the

abundance of many wicked.

For the arms of the wicked shall be broken, but Yahweh

upholds the righteous.

— Psalm 37:16-17

"The Spirit of the Lord is on me,

because he has anointed me to preach good news to

the poor.

He has sent me to heal the broken hearted,

to proclaim release to the captives,

recovering of sight to the blind,

to deliver those who are crushed,

and to proclaim the acceptable year of the Lord."

— Luke 4:18-19

So does that mean that those who are rich are more wicked than those who are poor? It is a common belief today, with it not being seen as too radical to say, "Eat the rich". It is hard to imagine that people (and the specifics come to mind freely: Bezos, Musk, Gates, Buffett, Zuckerberg) can attain such extreme wealth as they have without crossing some moral or ethical boundaries (ones which I would certainly never cross!). And who are the rich? For most people, it does not include themselves. In 1971, political hopeful Bernie Sanders said he thought it was "immoral" for half of the United States Senate to be composed of millionaires who are supposed to be serving as representatives of the people of their states, the average of whom was certainly not a millionaire. When he later became a millionaire senator, he then began to say, rather, "billionaires shouldn't exist". This may be principled consistency on the basis of inflation, or it may be consistent on the basis that all of us tend to covet more and more of what we do not have, and believe ourselves to be more righteous than perhaps we actually are.

Yet despite having obvious care for the poor, the Bible is not so quick to cast the rich and the wicked as being the same person. There are many examples of the richest also being the most righteous, whether a person recorded in history or an archetypal character in the wisdom literature: Joseph was the second most rich and powerful person in Egypt (Genesis 41); Job was both "blameless and upright" and "the greatest of all the children of the east" (Job 1) based on his large number of possessions; and in Proverbs 11:24, the "wise one" either starts or ends rich by being generous with his possessions, while the "fool" is stingy and becomes poor, if he was not already poorer to begin with:

There is one who scatters, and increases yet more.

There is one who withholds more than is appropriate, but gains poverty.

Then, there are three interesting passages in Luke that are worth studying to see what they say about money and they are a bit hard to place in any of the previous categories. One is a narrative of the story of Zacchaeus, a tax collector who had previously defrauded others by collecting more tax than they owed for his own benefit (Luke 19:1-10). After meeting Jesus, having his heart changed, and repenting of his wrong behavior, he vowed to repay those he harmed back four times, in line with the punishment for stealing sheep (Exodus 22:1) and mirroring the story of David's judgment for sheep theft (2 Samuel 12:6) (interesting to note, there are numerous punishments for different circumstances; for example, in some circumstances described in Leviticus 6:1-7, it is appropriate to pay back what was stolen plus an additional 20%. Zacchaeus seems to have chosen to pay back 400%, even though that was not the explicit requirement for what he had done. Obvious to some, but obvious in the other direction to others, paying back four times what you stole does not seem to be a rule. The principle repeated throughout the Bible is that money obtained unjustly is rotten, and a heart renewed by Christ will be different and seek renewal to what is not rotten.)

The second interesting passage worth studying is a parable describing a shrewd manager about to lose his job (Luke 16:1-15). He goes behind his master's back to decrease the debt of those who owe to his master, thereby earning the favor of the debtors while seeming to cheat his master of what he is owed. The parable does not imply that his master is an unfair man, and so we cannot understand the commendation for the shrewd manager's actions as righting the wrongs of his master (and, this understanding is even more strained by the fact the commendation came from the master. Would we trust his moral judgment if he was the immoral character of the story?). The Bible elsewhere is clear that these "false balances" the manager is using are abominations to God (Proverbs 11:1), and that does not change in this parable. It is easier to avoid worrying about what the shrewd manager is doing by focusing on how Jesus explains the parable. According to him, the summary is to "use worldly wealth to gain friends for yourselves, so that when it is gone, you will be welcomed into eternal dwellings." This parable exhorts his followers to spend as much effort on attaining heavenly rewards as more "earthly" people spend on attaining earthly rewards. As a corollary, this excludes his followers, the children of the light, from spending as much effort on attaining earthly rewards as do others.

The third interesting passage worthy of your time is also found in Luke 16. This is another parable, dealing with a poor beggar named Lazarus, and a rich man (19-31). Both die, and where the poor man suffered in life, and the rich man lived in comfort, the roles are now reversed. The rich man begs to be able to tell his family, warning them to change their ways in life so as not to suffer his same fate. We must look to the consistent message of Jesus to see what he is asking us to take from this parable. Is the focus of this parable on our actions, telling us to make a good transaction to properly balance our level of comfort and suffering in this life with the next (a daunting task, considering Jesus promises eternal life)? Or should our focus be on our hearts and how to change them, and the internal and external circumstances of both comfort and suffering will then follow?

Finally, as much as the "health and wealth" promised by what is called "The Prosperity Gospel" is false, and a result of eisegesis, there is a reason proponents of this alternative gospel believe in it. It would be incomplete not to include examples of passages which show righteous people who trust God being rewarded with wealth and unrighteous people punished with poverty.

> Bring the whole tithe into the storehouse, that there may be food in my house, and test me now in this," says Yahweh of Armies, "if I will not open you the windows of heaven, and pour you out a blessing, that there will not be room enough for.
>
> — Malachi 3:10
>
> Your substance and your treasures will I give for a spoil without price, and that for all your sins, even in all your borders.
>
> — Jeremiah 15:13

But for further completeness, compare again to the story of Job, a righteous man who loses all of his wealth, or Psalm 73, which describes the wicked, who "being always at ease, they increase in riches". Yet both Job and Psalm 73 end in a similar way: "But it is good for me to come close to God. I have made the Lord Yahweh my refuge, that I may tell of all your works".

Beyond this general understanding of how money is discussed in the Bible, there is a specific moral imperative related to money for Christians. This imperative is discussed briefly in the book *The Moral Vision of the New Testament*, and we will discuss it here as well.

Beyond the Righteousness of the Scribes and Pharisees

Before beginning, though, a brief warning based on the teachings of Jesus. From reading the Sermon the Mount in Matthew 5-7, it seems that Jesus does not care only for right action from his followers, but rather (or more importantly, and sequentially first) a right heart. Sure, Jesus' followers should not murder (Matthew 5:21, quoting Exodus 20:13). "But I tell you that everyone who is angry with his brother without a cause will be in danger of the judgment." (Matthew 5:22)

Withholding from murder is described as the righteousness of the scribes and Pharisees (Matthew 5:20). Withholding from murder of your brother in your heart is what is asked of you in order to go beyond this basic, minimum level of righteousness, and so "enter into the Kingdom of Heaven".

And so a similar concept is at play with all of Jesus' commandments to his followers. Many, Christian and non-Christian alike, hear the commands and believe they are necessary to follow in order for Jesus to like them, or to gain their salvation into the afterlife, or to transform the world into utopia. None of these are the case. Rather, the goal of the Christian, the little Christ, is to become more like Christ, observing and following his teaching as the apprentice observes the master, living as the Christ would live if He were you; and this begins on the inside. Jesus is calling us beyond legalism, the joy of lawyers in carving out loopholes for themselves and their clients. We should not be asking "what is the bare minimum I can do in order to still be following Jesus?", but rather, "what can I do to fully join you, Jesus, who is all powerful and worthy, in your redemptive project for the world and its inhabitants, and how can I increase my faith to do so?"

The Bible in Support of Financial Interdependence

With commentary, what follows are passages of the Bible which cast a vision for the new community of Christians on how best to acclimate to being a citizen in the Kingdom of God, specifically as it pertains to money and how we use it for our brothers' and sisters' benefits. We must allow that in the new heavens and the new earth described in the Bible, it is possible that we will not have a white picket fence around our mortgaged house, even though we have one where we live now, and so it is possible it is not worth learning to love these things too much. It is also possible there are things far more worthy of our love that we will be shaped to love and be given as we seek them.

Matthew 18:12-35 contains parables of Jesus describing the generosity, forgiveness, and self-sacrifice that is inherent to the character of God. The imperative here is that if God is so ultimately generous with us, where Jesus died for us to forgive us our sins and reconcile Himself to us, we are now free to be at least a portion as generous to others.

Matthew 25:31-4 contains the parable of dividing the sheep from the goats, where one goes to eternal life, and the other to eternal punishment, on the basis of how one treats the hungry, the thirsty, the stranger, the sick, and the prisoner, and therefore, how one treats Jesus Himself. ("Most certainly I tell you, because you didn't do it to one of the least of these, you didn't do it to me.")

Below is a passage from Mark:

> As he was going out into the way, one ran to him, knelt before him, and asked him, "Good Teacher, what shall I do that I may inherit eternal life?"
>
> Jesus said to him, "Why do you call me good? No one is good except one—God. You know the commandments: 'Do not murder,' 'Do not commit adultery,' 'Do not steal,' 'Do not give false testimony,' 'Do not defraud,' 'Honor your father and mother.'"
>
> He said to him, "Teacher, I have observed all these things from my youth."
>
> Jesus looking at him loved him, and said to him, "One thing you lack. Go, sell whatever you have, and give to the poor, and you will have treasure in heaven; and come, follow me, taking up the cross."

But his face fell at that saying, and he went away sorrowful, for he was one who had great possessions.

— Mark 10:17-22

Two errors are common in reading this passage. One, that because Jesus called this specific man to give up all of his possessions that Jesus is calling all Christians to give up all of their possessions. And two, that because Jesus was directing this command to this one specific man, that Jesus will never again ask one of his followers the same thing.

Many who care deeply about the condition of the poor of this world love the book of Luke because of how often it speaks for them and indicts the rich to incline their hearts towards them:

He has put down princes from their thrones,

and has exalted the lowly.

He has filled the hungry with good things.

He has sent the rich away empty.

He has given help to Israel, his servant, that he might remember mercy,

as he spoke to our fathers,

to Abraham and his offspring forever."

— Luke 1:52-55

Now great multitudes were going with him. He turned and said to them, "If anyone comes to me, and doesn't disregard his own father, mother, wife, children, brothers, and sisters, yes, and his own life also, he can't be my disciple. Whoever doesn't bear his own cross, and come after me, can't be my disciple. For which of you, desiring to build a tower, doesn't first sit down and count the cost, to see if he has enough to complete it? Or perhaps, when he has laid a foundation, and is not able to finish, everyone who sees begins to mock him, saying, 'This man began to build, and wasn't able to finish.' Or what king, as he goes to encounter another king in war, will not sit down first and consider whether he is able with ten thousand to meet him who comes against him with twenty thousand? Or else, while the other is yet a great way off, he sends an envoy, and asks for conditions of peace. So therefore whoever of you who doesn't renounce all that he has, he can't be my disciple. Salt is good, but if the salt becomes flat and tasteless, with what do you season it? It is fit neither for the soil nor for the manure pile. It is thrown out. He who has ears to hear, let him hear."

— Luke 14:25-35

A letter to the early church in Corinth urged its members to care for each other financially, drawing upon the concepts contained in the story of the manna in the wilderness in Exodus 16 listed previously.

For this is not that others may be eased and you distressed, but for equality. Your abundance at this present time supplies their lack, that their abundance also may become a supply for your lack; that there may be equality. As it is written, "He who gathered much had nothing left over, and he who gathered little had no lack."

— 2 Corinthians 8:13-15

A similar exhortation to care for other Christians is written in the letter to the church in Philippi...

If therefore there is any exhortation in Christ, if any consolation of love, if any fellowship of the Spirit, if any tender mercies and compassion, make my joy full by being like-minded, having the same love, being of one accord, of one mind; doing nothing through rivalry or through conceit, but in humility, each counting others better than himself; each of you not just looking to his own things, but each of you also to the things of others.

— Philippians 2:4

...and in the letter 1 John.

But whoever has the world's goods and sees his brother in need, then closes his heart of compassion against him, how does God's love remain in him?

> My little children, let's not love in word only, or with the tongue only, but in deed and truth.
>
> — 1 John 3:17-18

Finally, consider the early church described in Acts in the epigraph, and observe how many other churches are encouraged to follow this same model.

The Bible Against Financial Interdependence

It is not convincing, and people may believe you are trying to hide something, if you share only those passages which seem to agree with what you want to say and no passages that raise doubts or seem to directly contradict you. Even if not directly malicious, ignoring these passages might still result in eisegesis, leading to a false understanding.

One such passage records Jesus, saying,

> For you always have the poor with you, and whenever you want to, you can do them good; but you will not always have me.
>
> — Mark 14:17

The idea here is that Jesus is deprioritizing caring for the poor, and instead prioritizing himself for his disciples. And if we believe Jesus is trustworthy, this is the correct priority order.

But we fall in danger if we view this as "lower the priority of caring for the poor", instead of the proper "raise the priority of caring for Jesus". First, Jesus does not say do not care for the poor, and in fact says, "whenever you want to, you can do them good." It is also important to compare this verse to verses in Deuteronomy 15:1-11, which describe a provision for how Israel should manage debts.

In verses 4-5 of this passage in Deuteronomy, it says, "However, there need be no poor people among you, for in the land the Lord your God is giving you to possess as your inheritance, he will richly bless you, if only you fully obey the Lord your God and are careful to follow all these commands I am giving you today." And yet in verse 11, it says again, "There will always be poor people in the land. Therefore I command you to be openhanded toward your fellow Israelites who are poor and needy in your land."

Instead of being a verse against financial interdependence, it only further confirms it.

Financial Interdependence in Practice

With the way the world is set up, it seems almost impossible to live up to the challenge the Bible presents (and Mark 10:27 comes to mind). Our money is set up in retirement accounts, or stored away to make payments on mortgage and rent, or already accounted for to pay for health insurance. Our situation is only more complex than in the ancient world, but not really all that different. Trust in the supposed safety of money today is the same as trust in the supposed safety of money yesterday. Jesus may very well ask us to "sell whatever you have and give to the poor" in order to break the spell that money has on us and so we can freely follow him.

But it seems foolish to do this. Shouldn't a wise Christian be a good steward of what they have? Isn't it wise to save for your future and so not be a burden on others, and isn't it wise to pay for health insurance so that if a medical disaster strikes, you do not lose your house and make your family destitute to pay for it? Wouldn't a wise Christian not be married, because some marriages end in divorce, and so much heartache and many financial woes could be avoided? To entangle ourselves with others is messy business, and our relationship with Jesus might be the messiest of them all. He comes to us bloodied and beaten, and yet longs for us to be with him. This entanglement is exactly what the Bible calls for in the new Christian community, a new family formed through our shared adoption by God.

A few examples of what this interdependence might look like have been hinted at. Rather than trusting in the stock market to provide for our care in our later years, we can trust in our families and our extended Christian family to care for us, as we have in centuries past. Health insurance is one of the scariest things for people to give up, but you must remember Christians invented the hospital and the idea of medically caring for others on a mass scale. Already, health insurance is like a reverse lottery ticket: you pay tens of thousands of dollars per year with the hope that when you need money, it is there to cover you, but you also hope you never have to use it. Like all casinos, the numbers work out where the house always wins. If more people were taking money than paying money to the insurance company, the insurance company would be out of business and unable to pay for anymore Super Bowl commercials. In the United States, between the years 2010 and 2018, in attempting to reform parts of the health care system, people were fined with extra taxes for failing to carry health insurance. This was to avoid a "death spiral", where only the sickest would carry insurance, shedding the less sick from the insurance pool as premiums for coverage rise higher and higher. It is necessary for healthy people who require little medical care to subsidize costs for the more sick. This talk of "death spirals" is not a political talking point against certain policies for health insurance, but a logical and real outcome describing human behavior arising from an unforgiven heart. A Christian, fully mature, would be able to give money for the medical care of another even when the costs do not benefit them, and would not require the force and threat of a government's fines and jails to do so.

There is a lot of talk these days in politics (and therefore, everyday speech) about how to make amends for past injustices. There is no doubt these injustices occurred, but efforts trying to correct them have gotten mired down. Christians believe that Satan loves situations like this. An injustice has occurred, and now in trying to correct the injustice new divisions arise. Christians also believe God will ultimately mete out perfect justice based on his character, giving everyone exactly what they deserve (a scary thought!) But God is also merciful, and so he will withhold some of what people deserve. How this will shake out is beyond any human knowledge, and should also not be counted among someone's daily anxieties. Psalm 37 is useful here.

I want to float one such idea for a way Christians can begin to seek unity and confront historic and ongoing injustice, but I leave the door open for even better ideas. Churches can act as a conduit to allow people to claim reparations for past wrongs if they were wronged in a way that cannot be repaid through normal means (for example, confronting another directly or through the court system), or to pay reparations if they feel like they have benefitted unjustly relative to others. It can start small and scale larger. In my idea for such a scheme, individuals contribute money to a pot based on how much they feel they have benefited unjustly monetarily, and individuals also make claims to shares to that pot (for example, a number 0-100) if they feel they have been treated unjustly. An individual can (and probably should!) both contribute and make claims, for in the course of life you surely hurt and are hurt by others in ways that are impossible to quantify. The total pot is then split into the total number of shares and distributed based on how the shares are claimed. This can repeat so long as people are willing to contribute and willing to claim shares, and it can expand along city blocks and neighborhoods. One particular geographic area may have more people who believe they have unjustly benefitted from the economic systems of the world, or one area may have more people who believe they have been unjustly harmed; the goal would be to have a good mix of both, and for complete impartiality and fairness should ultimately encompass everyone in the world. The great thing is no one is required to contribute and no one is automatically and unwillingly labeled as a victim. The origin of the movement of wealth from actual and so-called oppressors to victims and so-called victims is not outside of individuals, but inside individual hearts, which comports with the principles of the coming Kingdom of Heaven. In addition, real victims in societies can be compensated and have their worldly needs met, and Christians can be satisfied that God will deal justly with anyone perpetrating new injustices by falsely claiming more shares than they are due relative to another. Of course, I say it is a "great thing", but another greater idea surely exists.

I want to encourage Christians not to fail to implement an idea that mirrors Biblical principles for fear that it will not work "in the real world". The "real world" and its values are upside-down compared to the Kingdom of Heaven, so much so that what we call "the real world" obscurs what is really real. Remember, Satan was once called "the prince of this world" (John 12:31). The author of *The Moral Vision of the New Testament* describes how he and his wife lived for five years in a community called Metanoia Fellowship which sought to have "all things in common" as in Acts 2:44, and yet this community failed. Who knows why such a thing failed? If we determine the Bible shows a particular vision of morality, are we in a good position to judge it? When it fails, was the Bible wrong, and what share of the fault lies with us?

Financial Interdependence in Art

Sometimes it is hard to imagine something in practice before it exists. Surely, the examples of church communities in history who have lived up to the high standard for money management and communal interdependence described in the Bible are seen as extraordinary exceptions rather than the norm. The norm, by comparison, is well below this standard.

Art helps expand the imagination, whether this art is music, literature, poetry, movies, painting, or sculpture. Alexander Solzhenitsyn has a helpful perspective on this in his Nobel Prize speech from 1970.

I would like to consider *It's a Wonderful Life* to better understand financial interdependence. What follows are spoilers, for anyone who has not yet had a chance to watch it. In this film, George Bailey lives a deeply meaningful life by all accounts: it has its highs, it has its lows; sometimes things turn out way better than he could hope for, and yet he is still often frustrated at his relatively modest accomplishments and many missed opportunities. When he wanted to travel the world, he instead had to stay behind to run his father's mortgage lending business. Later, on the day of his wedding, when he was counting a large stack of money given as wedding gifts and dreaming with his new bride of their honeymoon adventures, he again had to forego the opportunity to leave his hometown, instead loaning his wedding money to clients in order to spare them and his business during a Great Depression-era bank run. His frustration reaches its climax when his uncle, one of his business partners, misplaces a large sum of money at the same time that a no-nonsense bank inspector is visiting them. George Bailey considers suicide, but this is where the movie turns around, and with the help of a plot device named Clarence he is able to see what the world would have been like without his influence.

His character is contrasted with that of Mr. Potter, a fat cat banker. When George's business partner misplaced the money, Mr. Potter found it, and yet he did not return it, hoping instead George would lose his business. In the version of the world without George Bailey, many people who were previously living enjoyable and meaningful lives were not. People who were generous and trusting were now bitter and cynical. A successful pharmacist was instead a destitute alcoholic. One main difference between George and Mr. Potter was that George cared for others, both financially and otherwise, even and especially if it meant self-sacrifice, while Mr. Potter embodied the ultimate in financial independence, caring only for himself. The movie reaches its triumphant climax when George returns to his home, no longer wishing to die but instead be with his family on Christmas Eve, and he is soon followed by a procession of everyone in town whose lives he has touched, and they bring more than enough money to keep his business afloat. His brother (who would have died had George not existed), exclaims, "A toast to my big brother George, the richest man in town!" While Mr. Potter can trust in his own coffers, as far as money can be trusted, to provide for his needs, he has no friends. George, meanwhile, is friends with everyone (less one) in town, and his material needs are provided for just as much as Mr. Potter's. Interdependence does not mean lack; in fact, those who are able to rely on others may have more.

This movie also addresses another point. Some believe that liberation from the evils of money can only be achieved by transforming things at the level of society: certain laws are unjust, or only under certain forms of governments can the meaningful things in life flourish. This has a kernel of truth: some laws are unjust, and some forms of government are worse than others. But both George Bailey and Mr. Potter are living and working in a capitalistic society which prioritizes earning money by its nature, and yet still the individual is the axis through which the world and its values are flipped. All would not be well if only we dismantled capitalism, or if only we eliminated government interference in free trade to fully embrace capitalism unhindered. Imagine a society given perfect laws, and yet the government and her citizens were populated with people with imperfect hearts confident in their own righteousness; a nation of Mr. Potters. These laws would not restrain these people for very long. The life and story of Alexander Solzhenitsyn is again relevant: Stalin tried to bring to his nation the utopia promised by Lenin through Marx, and instead unleashed hell. Let us not be naive.

In discussing financial interdependence, many either decry it or praise it as socialism, depending on one's preferred politics. Some say Jesus himself was a socialist. To these people, I say: What part of "Repent, for the Kingdom of Heaven is at hand" did you not understand? What do you think of the wealth distribution described in the Parable of the Talents? The Gospel is a message of changing hearts and in correctly understanding reality, not a handbook for changing state constitutions and economic policy. Jesus counted among his apostles religious zealots who sought the violent overthrow of the Roman government; this is not the path he chose. He also counted among his apostles tax collectors who, even if not outright supportive, collaborated with oppressive Roman rule; Jesus did not affirm this either. If Jesus can be labeled on our terms, using our words instead of letting him speak, he is a monarchist, and he is King.

Interdependence with All, or only Fellow Believers?

It is an interesting question. As shown on previous pages, the Bible places special emphasis on care of the poor, while also giving examples where the poor are to be treated no differently (for example, in Exodus 30:15 and Leviticus 19:15). But are poor Christians to be treated differently than poor non-believers?

The idea makes sense. What would society think of parents who allow their own children to go hungry, while spending all of their money to care for orphans (I do not think this is a common problem)? Obviously, one should care for their family, and you would worry about their motives if they cared for others more. The Bible uses the language of family to describe the new community of believers and their relationship with God.

For as many as are led by the Spirit of God, these are children of God. For you didn't receive the spirit of bondage again to fear, but you received the Spirit of adoption, by whom we cry, "Abba! Father!" The Spirit himself testifies with our spirit that we are children of God.

— Romans 8:14-16

There are a number of verses, including the previously referenced 2 Corinthians 8:13-15, Philippians 2:4, and 1 John 3:17-18 that seem to point to the idea that Christians should first make sure there are no poor among themselves (both in their immediate household and also in the community of believers) before attempting to bless the wider world. The case is stated strongly in 1 Timothy, and plainly in Galatians.

But if anyone doesn't provide for his own, and especially his own household, he has denied the faith, and is worse than an unbeliever.

— 1 Timothy 5:8

For he who sows to his own flesh will from the flesh reap corruption. But he who sows to the Spirit will from the Spirit reap eternal life. Let's not be weary in doing good, for we will reap in due season, if we don't give up. So then, as we have opportunity, let's do what is good toward all men, and especially toward those who are of the household of the faith.

— Galatians 6:8-10

Similar to Mark 14:7, I believe the instruction is not to care about the global poor less; rather, care about the Christian poor more and so set your priorities in right order. This makes implicit and perfect sense if you rightly understand other Christians as members of your family, or even as other members of the same body (as in Romans 12), and quickly becomes non-controversial except among the most perverse.

So, This is All a Scam, Right?

The examples of people using the Bible or other supposed divine revelation to achieve excessive worldly comfort are numerous. Both the earnest and the swindlers will say similar things, so how do you know who is who? Perhaps no one among the leaders and preachers of Christianity actually believe its message to be true, but have recognized it as a particularly effective grift to part the gullible and cutely dumb masses from their money. Or perhaps some members of the congregation claim to be Christians only to receive financial support so they can rest and not work so hard? A similar theme I restate: such errors can be avoided by all by properly exegeting the Bible, and God will bring His perfect judgment to all so that we need not worry ourselves about what others do in the long run.

It is helpful to look at the earliest teachers of Christianity to see how lucrative of a grift it really is. Sometimes, the case is made that preachers should be rightly compensated for the work of preaching; if they collapse from lack of eating, they cannot preach for long, no matter how much self-sacrifice is at the center of the message.

Remain in that same house, eating and drinking the things they give, for the laborer is worthy of his wages. Don't go from house to house. Into whatever city you enter, and they receive you, eat the things that are set before you.

— Luke 10:7-8

But let him who is taught in the word share all good things with him who teaches.

— Galatians 6:6

In other cases, it seems the preachers took special care to not require monetary compensation for preaching so that it did not become a stumbling block for the message.

For you remember, brothers, our labor and travail; for working night and day, that we might not burden any of you, we preached to you the Good News of God.

— 1 Thessalonians 2:9

For you know how you ought to imitate us. For we didn't behave ourselves rebelliously among you neither did we eat bread from anyone's hand without paying for it, but in labor and travail worked night and day, that we might not burden any of you, not because we don't have the right, but to make ourselves an example to you, that you should imitate us. For even when we were with you, we commanded you this: "If anyone is not willing to work, don't let him eat." For we hear of some who walk among you in rebellion, who don't work at all, but are busybodies. Now those who are that way, we command and exhort in the Lord Jesus Christ, that they work with quietness and eat their own bread.

— 2 Thessalonians 3:7-12

But how does one decide when it is appropriate to request money, and when it is not? Does it depend on the financial state of the ones you are preaching to, or on your own need at any given time? There does not seem be a well defined set of legal requirements, but rather, the principle that it seems to depend on the maturity of the believers you are preaching to, with more mature Christians being exhorted to exist in a community of financial interdependence, while immature Christians are not yet held to that standard (though that is the direction they are being nudged).

Or did I commit a sin in humbling myself that you might be exalted, because I preached to you God's Good News free of charge? I robbed other assemblies, taking wages from them that I might serve you. When I was present with you and was in need, I wasn't a burden on anyone, for the brothers, when they came from Macedonia, supplied the measure of my need. In everything I kept myself from being burdensome to you, and I will continue to do so.

— 2 Corinthians 11:7-9

You yourselves also know, you Philippians, that in the beginning of the Good News, when I departed from Macedonia, no assembly shared with me in the matter of giving and receiving but you only. For even in Thessalonica you sent once and again to my need. Not that I seek for the gift, but I seek for the fruit that increases to your account. But I have all things, and abound. I am filled, having received from Epaphroditus the things that came from you, a sweet-smelling fragrance, an acceptable and well-pleasing sacrifice to God. My God will supply every need of yours according to his riches in glory in Christ Jesus.

— Philippians 4:15-19

Note, Paul is being funny and hyperbolic in saying he "robbed" other believers. See also 1 Corinthians 9 and Acts 20:17-38 for extended handlings of this topic, and consider also the history of the Christian martyrs following in the steps of Jesus to determine if they really believed in the message or were only involved for the benefits.

Coming to the end, let us finish as does Ecclesiastes, deriving its conclusion by examining all possible options for how best to find meaning in life, and whether or not it comes from money, wisdom, pleasure, power, or something else.

This is the end of the matter. All has been heard. Fear God and keep his commandments; for this is the whole duty of man. For God will bring every work into judgment, with every hidden thing, whether it is good, or whether it is evil.

— Ecclesiastes 12:13-14

Summary

- The Bible talks a lot about money and portrays a consistent way of how to think about and use it

- Christians are called to a high standard of communal living that they usually do not meet

- Christians should not be first concerned with their actions related to money, but rather their relationship with Jesus and their beliefs about him and what he says about money

Questions for thinking

1. Do you think the Bible is univocal about money, or does it say contradictory things?
2. Richard Hayes, the author of *The Moral Vision of the New Testament*, says, "For the church to heed the New Testament's challenge on the question of possessions would require nothing less than a new Reformation." Do you agree?
3. Is someone a Christian if they do not share their possessions?

Chapter Three

Discipleship Everyday

"Everyone therefore who hears these words of mine and does them, I will liken him to a wise man who built his house on a rock. The rain came down, the floods came, and the winds blew and beat on that house; and it didn't fall, for it was founded on the rock. Everyone who hears these words of mine and doesn't do them will be like a foolish man who built his house on the sand. The rain came down, the floods came, and the winds blew and beat on that house; and it fell—and its fall was great."

— Matthew 7:24-27

"Go and make disciples of all nations, baptizing them in the name of the Father and of the Son and of the Holy Spirit, teaching them to observe all things that I commanded you. Behold, I am with you always, even to the end of the age." Amen.

— Matthew 28:19-20

THIS BOOK IS PRIMARILY about money, but the Bible is not; nor was it Jesus' main message during his earthly ministry. Therefore, this chapter will not be about money, but rather about how to carry out what I claim is the moral imperative about how to handle money. While the FIRE movement tells its followers to look to the horizon of the future and seek early retirement to live the kind of life you want before it is too late, the message of Jesus is that your life is just beginning, so come to Him to learn how best to live it. Rather than spending our time and money to Retire Early, I propose instead we use our time for Discipleship Everyday.

So how do we as Christians do that? The same way we learn to love our enemies. It is not a "fake it 'til you make it" scenario, where you perform like an actor and hope to eventually catch up with it. Looking at how well the average person sticks to a New Year's Resolution, I would guess that most people would give up and grow resentful before they achieve their goal. Rather, we start with the belief that Jesus is a smart person who gives good advice, then we follow his commandments, praying that the Holy Spirit will change our hearts so that we are able to do so. The first step is harder and rarer than you would imagine among Christians.

What if we could convince, trick, scare, or guilt every Christian into giving a large sum of money (say, $10,000) for the alleviation of poverty and meeting others' physical needs? Would the effect be huge, or would not much be changed? Now, imagine we exhort Christians to give money proportional to the size of their faith (with some giving pennies, and some giving none at all), but then we work on helping them grow as disciples of Jesus and in growing their faith. Anyone loyal to the FIRE lifestyle will have an easy time answering this question: would you rather have a lump sum of $10,000, or would you rather have a smaller pot of money continuously and ever increasingly added to? Imagine this pot subjected to compounding interest over 30 years. Now imagine this pot compounded for eternity, and understand that we are talking about the state of believers' faith.

We're All Disciples of Someone

Disciples are people who follow another to learn how to live their life. The word "disciple" seems somewhat archaic and lofty, and so perhaps a more helpful and understandable word is "apprentice". Being a disciple or apprentice is not just a matter of filling up on knowledge and facts, though that will happen, but is a more holistic relationship of learning what kind of person to be and how to become that person. The first people that disciple us are usually our parents. As we grow, we may learn from other relatives, our neighbors, our teachers, and our friends. Perhaps in another time, or in another culture, our bosses at work would disciple us, but I don't think right now that is particularly prevalent. Instead, we are discipled by celebrities, politicians, and media outlets who shape the way we think about ourselves and others. Discipleship usually happens by convenience: wherever or whomever we spend the most time with is where and by whom we are discipled. Christians claim to be discipled by Christ, but how often do they spend time reading the Bible or learning to live a Christian life by spending time with a more mature Christian, and how much time do we spend consuming movies, news stories with an agenda, or reading and participating in outraged arguments on social media? To choose to be discipled by another takes a concerted effort to spend time with that person, and sometimes a concerted effort to avoid others. You are always being discipled by others, whether you think you are or want to be or not.

Disciples and Converts

I said that Christians "claim" to be discipled by Christ, implying not everyone is. Isn't discipleship to Jesus inherent in being a Christian? It seems there is some confusion between being a disciple and being a convert.

A disciple learns how to live a life that Jesus would if He were you. They observe, listen, and act. Note, this is not to say that the salvation Jesus offers and His forgiveness of sin depends on your action. Jesus has already finished this work. Instead, living like Jesus is the fruit of a repentant heart, showing the wisdom in both "hearing" and "doing" (Matthew 7:24). Disciples are commanded to "observe all the things I commanded you" (Matthew 28:20). In comparison, a convert is one who mentally assents to the message of Christianity, one who confesses with their mouth that Jesus is Lord, but for some reason does not take seriously His messages regarding how to live one's life.

Why Would Someone Be a Convert?

Looking at history and the current landscape of Christians, does it seem that most live as if everything Jesus said was true? Do they love their enemies in the face of unjust treatment? Do they live as if their life is eternal, and their possessions are perishable?

Some are content to accept the blood of Jesus for the forgiveness of sins. Others want to take the teachings that agree with them or their political party, but ignore those teachings which are not ascendantly popular. Both groups share the fact that they do not want to become entangled with the person of Jesus; they want the parts they want, and not the parts that require what they see as work or sacrifice.

It is possible some Christians do not believe aspects of the Christian story; admittedly, it is a stretch to believe that a man was God, died, and rose from the dead when you have never seen something like that happen before. On the other hand, if you do believe that, and think him reliable when he said that would happen, wouldn't it make sense to follow what he says in other areas? Perhaps some Christians do not think he is reliable or smart. He was alive 2,000 years ago, and we have learned so much more since then! Or perhaps other Christians are afraid of appearing weird or stupid to others. Again, if you believe there was a man who claimed to be God and proved it by returning from death, how much can you care about what others think? The fear the apostles felt after the crucifixion of Jesus disappeared when he returned bodily to them and let them place their hands upon his wounds.

The primary difference between those content with converting to Christianity and those seeking deeper and deeper discipleship is belief. People's actions give insight into their beliefs, despite what their words may speak. If someone says they believe eating well and exercising is important for their health, but they do not do these things, what do they really believe? Either they do not believe what they said strongly enough to act on it, or there is some other belief at work countering their ability to act; perhaps they do not believe they are worthy of having a body well-taken care of? The same is true of improving your spiritual health, which a life in Jesus produces. If you observe Jesus' life and words and see that he prays, rests, worships, plays, works, spends time with others, and spends time alone with God, and you do not do these things, what beliefs about these things are at work in you?

Do you believe Jesus is smart, trustworthy, and knowledgeable? Do you believe Jesus is a liar? Do you believe Jesus is God? Do you believe God is worthy of worship? If not, what or who is worthy of worship?

The Bible in Support of Discipleship Everyday

The life of a Christian is not a sedentary one. Every Christian was a sinner, and still is one, but they are not to remain that way. There is a direction in Christian life, turning away from sin and turning towards holiness, the *metanoia* (repentance) preached by Jesus. What follows is a collection of passages from the Bible supporting the idea that discipleship, and specifically discipleship everyday, is the path for Christians who submit themselves to the works of the Holy Spirit.

> But seek first God's Kingdom and his righteousness; and all these things will be given to you as well. Therefore don't be anxious for tomorrow, for tomorrow will be anxious for itself. Each day's own evil is sufficient.

> — Matthew 6:33-34

> You are my friends, if you do whatever I command you. No longer do I call you servants, for the servant doesn't know what his lord does. But I have called you friends, for everything that I heard from my Father, I have made known to you. You didn't choose me, but I chose you and appointed you, that you should go and bear fruit, and that your fruit should remain; that whatever you will ask of the Father in my name, he may give it to you.

> — John 15:14-16

For though you have ten thousand tutors in Christ, yet not many fathers. For in Christ Jesus, I became your father through the Good News. I beg you therefore, be imitators of me. Because of this I have sent Timothy to you, who is my beloved and faithful child in the Lord, who will remind you of my ways which are in Christ, even as I teach everywhere in every assembly.

— 1 Corinthians 4:15-17

Be imitators of me, even as I also am of Christ.

— 1 Corinthians 11:1

And this is just not a one-way street. Not only are we to be discipled by more mature Christians (as they, too, were discipled by more mature Christians, and they were discipled by Christ), but one day we will be the more mature Christian whose duty it is to disciple and make disciples.

The Bible Against Discipleship Everyday

To be believable, it is good to know and respond to evidence that seems to go against what you are trying to prove. I may have to write this section in a second edition of this booklet, because I cannot find any evidence which says discipleship everyday is not the desired path for every Christian. No where can I find where it says Jesus wishes to be crucified for Christians, but then leave them on their own. No where can I find where faith does not result in fruits of good works, changed character, and changed hearts.

The best use of this section is to increase this book's page count by one.

How to Become a Disciple

Despite being included in Jesus' Great Commission as he ascended to heaven, the project of creating disciples is not the main focus of churches today. Measurements are taken to determine how many people are filling seats on a Sunday, or else how Biblical literacy is trending over the years as measured by quizzes. Behind closed doors, tithe money is being counted. One of the difficulties in pursuing discipleship is that it is not countable in a results-oriented society. How do you know when you have achieved your goal, can check the box, and move on?

It is a similar question to how do you become a spouse? There is a one-time event, marriage, and then a lifetime of continually growing within a relationship with another. Even Jesus's closest followers were not "finished" when Jesus left them.

John 21 tells a story of Peter and Jesus reuniting after Jesus' death and resurrection. When they last parted, Peter had just told Jesus he would not abandon him, and would even die for him, but then he denied that he knew Jesus three times to others as soon as Jesus was arrested. This repetition of three is repeated in John 21, where Jesus asks Peter three times if he loves him. The parallel is clear, but an additional meaning is missed when reading this story in English. Other languages can better render the original Gree.

Jesus asks Peter, "Do you love (*agape*) me?", and Peter answers, "Yes, I love (*phileo*) you". Again, Jesus asks, "Do you love (*agape*) me?", and Peter answers again, "Yes, I love (*phileo*) you". Finally, Jesus changes the question, asking, "Do you love (*phileo*) me?", and Peter answers, "Yes, I love (*phileo*) you". In Spanish, the verbs used might be *amar* ('to love', a stronger love) and *querer* (a weaker kind of love, perhaps similar to 'to want'). *Agape* is a godly, self-sacrificial kind of love, but Peter was not yet ready for it. Jesus knew this and reached down to where Peter was in his weakness. Surely, Peter is a good role model, or is at least relatable, for us in our own vocation of discipleship.

But just as there is no one strict set of procedures for how to live and grow in a marriage relationship, there is no one repeatable path to discipleship. There are certainly wrong ways to go about both (for example, adultery, applied to both marriage and as used in the many biblical metaphors related to the fidelity of our relationship with God), but there are helpful general principles which can be applied. These principles include learning to love God, learning to know God, asking God to enter in and disciple you, deciding to become a disciple, and the mundane task of replacing old habits with new, healthier ones.

Love God

The apostle John described the Gospel, as compared to how I describe it at the beginning and end of this booklet, as follows:

> This is the message which we have heard from him and announce to you, that God is light, and in him is no darkness at all.
>
> — 1 John 1:5

Like a plant, we are disposed to seek the light for life. Everyone knows when they see good, and everyone knows when they see evil. When people claim that what is obviously evil is not, you know that even this is perverse. This tension is not a new one; the Bible makes mention of this as well (Roman 1:18-32 and through to Romans 2:1-11). God and His ways are inherently good, but if we do not understand this and actually believe it so that it influences our action, we have no motivation for following Him.

People seek truth and good as if these were inherently good things. The popularity of self-help books attest to this. No one, in trying to win converts to their political party, advertises themselves as the less virtuous option, even when the policy preferences of two political parties are exactly opposite and the other party claimed the same virtue first. Everyone seems to have an opinion on what is the best way to live. Christians are also have an opinion. So strong is their opinion that before the first believers were called Christians, they were said to be followers of The Way (not "a way"). They believe God is the ultimate good. John, in his mature years, understood this, and it was so important to him that it was his one sentence explanation of the Good News.

Know God

People rightly say that knowing biblical trivia is not a requirement for salvation. There will be no entrance exam to the new heaven and new earth that you must study for. But just like we would question a spousal relationship where one does not know the other's birthday, we would question how deep a Christian's relationship is with a God whose qualities and actions in history they do not know or understand. *Knowing God* by J. I. Packer is an appropriately titled book dealing with this topic in a lucid way that may be helpful for new Christians or as a reminder for old ones.

Memorizing verses from the Bible is often looked upon with scorn as a relic of the past, a punishment inflicted by fundamentalists upon the innocent. But if God truly is light, and there is no darkness in him, and all of Scripture is God-breathed, being able to draw upon the Bible no matter where you are or how well you can see or read is a powerful tool. It is like being in a dark cave with a flashlight with batteries that do not run dry, or with a torch that does not burn out. The alternative use for that space in your brain is for memorizing commercial jingles, movie quotes, and music lyrics.

Ask God

By this point, we know God more and better understand some of His attributes. One attribute is that God does not wish for anyone to taste death, as told by the Bible.

> Tell them, As I live, says the Lord Yahweh, I have no pleasure in the death of the wicked; but that the wicked turn from his way and live: turn, turn from your evil ways; for why will you die, house of Israel?
>
> — Ezekiel 33:11

But God is also holy, and unholy people cannot exist in relationship with Him, though he alone through the cross has the power to declare one holy (an interesting thought: for a God described by the Bible as the devouring fire [Isaiah 33:14], Dallas Willard posits, "the fires of heaven may well be hotter than the fires of hell"). But he does not force anyone to become holy who does not wish to, but rather he asks and leaves the door unlocked. And he wishes for us to ask, as well.

> Ask, and it will be given you. Seek, and you will find. Knock, and it will be opened for you.
>
> — Matthew 7:7

Decide to Follow Jesus

A wedding does not happen accidentally. Usually, a man proposes to a woman, and the woman accepts. A successful marriage does not happen accidentally, either. A lifetime of decisions are considered and made which either hurt or improve the marriage relationship. I hesitate to say "never", but I have not yet seen an exemplary marriage created without intentional investment and conscious decisions to act. Similarly, a commitment to a relationship with Jesus requires a choice and a lifetime of follow-up choices.

Much is made of the parable regarding "counting the cost" (Luke 14:28). It can make the whole business of following Jesus sound dreary and burdensome. This does not have to be so. Followers of the FIRE movement have counted the cost. They examined the costs of working in a career for 30 years in order to retire, and compared this to the costs of being more frugal and saving in order to retire earlier. They have decided, without a doubt, it is worth it to pursue FIRE. Most who are successful in achieving FIRE likely don't even consider it a sacrifice. It is, in fact, a much better way to live, and the payoff is much greater than the alternative.

Everyone who has left houses, or brothers, or sisters, or father, or mother, or wife, or children, or lands, for my name's sake, will receive one hundred times, and will inherit eternal life.

— Matthew 19:29

On the other hand, there is some component of counting the cost where it is still burdensome, at least so much as we are still burdened. Christians throughout the ages and in the world today are persecuted for believing in Jesus as opposed to what others say they should believe in. Jesus knows this.

If the world hates you, you know that it has hated me before it hated you. If you were of the world, the world would love its own. But because you are not of the world, since I chose you out of the world, therefore the world hates you.

— John 15:18-19

And as we said earlier, Jesus may yet ask us to give up our possessions much like the rich young ruler.

"Deciding" is a popular tactic of cults and cult-like political movements to increase membership and retention. If someone makes a public declaration, they are far less likely to back out for fear of ostracization or shame, or else they feel their costs are sunken. If you worry Christianity is a cult, do not decide to follow Jesus. "Deciding" is late on this list of actionable steps. Do you first believe God is lovable and worthy of love? Do you know something about who God is? Have you asked Him to change your heart and allow you to love him? Would you decide to marry someone without doing these first steps first? There is a reason there are so many marriage metaphors in the Bible. Do not marry someone who you think is, or who is, physically or emotionally abusive. Do not just become a convert and so risk joining a cult without actually reaping the benefits of said possible cult, nor fail to adhere to what this potential cult and its possible cult leader emphatically recommends its members do with their lives. Decide if you really believe Jesus is worth following before deciding to follow Him.

Replace Old Habits

If time spent together is required for discipleship, then the simple but impactful act of making more time to be discipled is profitable. This involves replacing old habits with new ones.

If you are not currently part of a church community, join one and become involved. If you do not pray, or read the Bible, take time you would otherwise spend watching TV or scrolling on your phone and use it for that. If, as we said, seeking truth is inherently good, it should be palatable to switch. Media, and especially social media, is not optimized for truth, but rather engagement with advertisers. If you must be shown outrageous lies or half-truths to reach that goal, so be it. Designers of these forms of media know how to create a product that results in addictive use, numbing a person's ability to be happy with less rewarding stimuli, and this is the more morally neutral aspect of social media. Social media has been used to foment genocide and to distract from genocide. It would be no great loss to use social media 10 or 15 minutes fewer per day, and a great gain to lose more.

Sabbath is seen as archaic as memorizing Bible verses. But the commandment to observe the Sabbath is listed alongside the commandments not to murder and not to covet what another has. If you took the Sabbath as seriously as the command to not murder, would you observe the Sabbath, or would there be more murders? I have found the Sabbath is a great gift. For me, the barrier to observing the Sabbath was one of changing beliefs (much like other barriers to discipleship). I needed to see the Sabbath as a gift of rest and opportunity to trust in God for my provisions instead of a restriction on my ability to accomplish tasks and make progress on projects or to store up comforts for myself. Rearranging work responsibilities so that one out of every seven days is not dedicated to work, but rather God, is another new habit recommended by the Bible.

The Holy Spirit

I think Christians are predisposed to giving less credit to the Holy Spirit than credit is due, from everything to having faith to believe in the good news of Jesus to one's ability to change their habits to better become a disciple. And so, this section is a brief reminder to not do that, with the brevity in inverse proportion to His role.

Jesus answered, "Very truly I tell you, no one can enter the kingdom of God unless they are born of water and the Spirit."

— John 3:5

However when he, the Spirit of truth, has come, he will guide you into all truth, for he will not speak from himself; but whatever he hears, he will speak. He will declare to you things that are coming.

— John 16:13

If Christ is in you, the body is dead because of sin, but the spirit is alive because of righteousness. But if the Spirit of him who raised up Jesus from the dead dwells in you, he who raised up Christ Jesus from the dead will also give life to your mortal bodies through his Spirit who dwells in you.

So then, brothers, we are debtors, not to the flesh, to live after the flesh. For if you live after the flesh, you must die; but if by the Spirit you put to death the deeds of the body, you will live.

— Romans 8:10-13

But the fruit of the Spirit is love, joy, peace, forbearance, kindness, goodness, faithfulness, gentleness and self-control. Against such things there is no law. Those who belong to Christ Jesus have crucified the flesh with its passions and desires. Since we live by the Spirit, let us keep in step with the Spirit. Let us not become conceited, provoking and envying each other.

— Galatians 5:22-26

Counting the Cost, Again

Still, after all of this, it may be hard to devote one's life to discipleship to Jesus. When one devotes themselves to the FIRE lifestyle in order to retire early, they know what they think they want to do with their future time. Looking to the future is just as important for the Christian. When building a fence and setting up fence posts, a straight line is only possible by starting with the first and final posts and placing the others in accordance. When Jesus says, "Come, follow me", only those with the largest of faith could do so without first asking, "Where are we going?"

Peter gives one answer:

> Blessed be the God and Father of our Lord Jesus Christ, who according to his great mercy caused us to be born again to a living hope through the resurrection of Jesus Christ from the dead, to an incorruptible and undefiled inheritance that doesn't fade away, reserved in Heaven for you, who by the power of God are guarded through faith for a salvation ready to be revealed in the last time.

— 1 Peter 1:4-5

Isaiah gives another:

> "For, behold, I create new heavens and a new earth;
>
> and the former things will not be remembered,
>
> nor come into mind.
>
> But be glad and rejoice forever in that which I create;
>
> for, behold, I create Jerusalem to be a delight,
>
> and her people a joy.
>
> I will rejoice in Jerusalem,
>
> and delight in my people;
>
> and the voice of weeping and the voice of crying

will be heard in her no more.

"No more will there be an infant who only lives a few days,

nor an old man who has not filled his days;

for the child will die one hundred years old,

and the sinner being one hundred years old will be accursed.

They will build houses and inhabit them.

They will plant vineyards and eat their fruit.

They will not build and another inhabit.

They will not plant and another eat:

for the days of my people will be like the days of a tree,

and my chosen will long enjoy the work of their hands.

They will not labor in vain

nor give birth for calamity;

for they are the offspring of Yahweh's blessed

and their descendants with them.

It will happen that before they call, I will answer;

and while they are yet speaking, I will hear.

The wolf and the lamb will feed together.

The lion will eat straw like the ox.

Dust will be the serpent's food.

They will not hurt nor destroy in all my holy mountain,"

says Yahweh.

— Isaiah 65:17-25

When I first heard the message of Jesus at the age of 21, I remember thinking, "This would be awesome, if it were true." But, at least I correctly recognized that the vision for the present and the future He presented was awesome. There is no scarcity, lack, or need of money or of time in the new heavens and new earth. I must ask: what, instead, would you rather choose to do with your retirement? All praise to Jesus for the opportunities he has prepared and secured for us.

Summary

- Everyone is discipled by someone and it usually based on time invested and proximity

- Christian communities often fail at discipling and being discipled, despite what the Bible says about it

- Discipleship is an active process, and Christians must choose to take time to read, pray, and live life and learn from more mature Christians

Questions for thinking

1. Where do Christians stray further from the high standards of the Bible: financial interdependence or discipleship?
2. What things need to change, both within you and outside of you, to lead to more successful discipleship?
3. Is FIDE biblical, and is it worth pursuing? What is the first practical thing you can begin doing, and does it fall under the category of FI or DE?

The Gospel

The gospel is the good news of Jesus.

Two thousand years ago, a boy was born in Bethlehem, in modern day Israel. When he grew up, he said, "Repent, for the Kingdom of Heaven is at hand!". That is: turn from your life without God, and enter reality as it really is, where God is present and approachable starting today. More than that, he said he also was God, somehow, and offered the one and only path to himself.

Through his death on the cross and his resurrection three days later, he proved the trustworthiness of what he said and he accomplished the sacrifice needed to reconcile sinful man with an utterly holy and praiseworthy God, welcoming all who believe in him into adoption into his family.

www.ingramcontent.com/pod-product-compliance
Lightning Source LLC
Chambersburg PA
CBHW072035150726
47999CB00002B/925